Building Real-Time Data Pipelines

Unifying Applications and Analytics with In-Memory Architectures

Conor Doherty, Gary Orenstein, Steven Camiña, and Kevin White

Beijing · Boston · Farnham · Sebastopol · Tokyo

Building Real-Time Data Pipelines

by Conor Doherty, Gary Orenstein, Steven Camiña, and Kevin White

Copyright © 2015 O'Reilly Media, Inc. All rights reserved.

Printed in the United States of America.

Published by O'Reilly Media, Inc., 1005 Gravenstein Highway North, Sebastopol, CA 95472.

O'Reilly books may be purchased for educational, business, or sales promotional use. Online editions are also available for most titles (*http://safaribooksonline.com*). For more information, contact our corporate/institutional sales department: 800-998-9938 or *corporate@oreilly.com*.

Editor: Marie Beaugureau	**Interior Designer:** David Futato
Production Editor: Kristen Brown	**Cover Designer:** Karen Montgomery
Copyeditor: Charles Roumeliotis	**Illustrator:** Rebecca Demarest

September 2015:   First Edition

Revision History for the First Edition

2015-09-02:   First Release

978-1-491-93547-7

[LSI]

Table of Contents

Introduction

Imagine you had a time machine that could go back one minute, or an hour. Think about what you could do with it. From the perspective of other people, it would seem like there was nothing you *couldn't* do, no contest you couldn't win.

In the real world, there are three basic ways to win. One way is to have something, or to know something, that your competition does not. Nice work if you can get it. The second way to win is to simply be more intelligent. However, the number of people who *think* they are smarter is much larger than the number of people who actually are smarter.

The third way is to process information faster so you can make and act on decisions faster. Being able to make more decisions in less time gives you an advantage in both information *and* intelligence. It allows you to try many ideas, correct the bad ones, and react to changes before your competition. If your opponent cannot react as fast as you can, it does not matter what they have, what they know, or how smart they are. Taken to extremes, it's almost like having a time machine.

An example of the third way can be found in high-frequency stock trading. Every trading desk has access to a large pool of highly intelligent people, and pays them well. All of the players have access to the same information at the same time, at least in theory. Being more or less equally smart and informed, the most active area of competition is the end-to-end speed of their decision loops. In recent years, traders have gone to the trouble of building their own wireless long-haul networks (*http://tabbforum.com/opinions/the-rise-of-next-gen-wireless-technology-in-financial-services?print_pre view=true&single=true*), to exploit the fact that microwaves move through the air 50% faster than light can pulse through fiber optics. This allows them to execute trades a crucial millisecond faster.

Finding ways to shorten end-to-end information latency is also a constant theme at leading tech companies. They are forever working to reduce the delay between something happening out there in the world or in their huge clusters of computers, and when it shows up on a graph. At Facebook in the early 2010s, it was normal to wait hours after pushing new code to discover whether everything was working efficiently. The full report came in the next day. After building their own distributed in-memory database and event pipeline, their information loop is now on the order of 30 seconds, and they push at least two full builds per day. Instead of slowing down as they got bigger, Facebook doubled down on making more decisions faster.

What is *your* system's end-to-end latency? How long is your decision loop, compared to the competition? Imagine you had a system that was twice as fast. What could you do with it? This might be the most important question for your business.

In this book we'll explore new models of quickly processing information end to end that are enabled by long-term hardware trends, learnings from some of the largest and most successful tech companies, and surprisingly powerful ideas that have survived the test of time.

—*Carlos Bueno*
Principal Product Manager at MemSQL,
author of The Mature Optimization Handbook
and Lauren Ipsum

CHAPTER 1

When to Use In-Memory Database Management Systems (IMDBMS)

In-memory computing, and variations of in-memory databases, have been around for some time. But only in the last couple of years has the technology advanced and the cost of memory declined enough that in-memory computing has become cost effective for many enterprises. Major research firms like Gartner have taken notice and have started to focus on broadly applicable use cases for in-memory databases, such as Hybrid Transactional/Analytical Processing (HTAP for short).

HTAP represents a new and unique way of architecting data pipelines. In this chapter we will explore how in-memory database solutions can improve operational and analytic computing through HTAP, and what use cases may be best suited to that architecture.

Improving Traditional Workloads with In-Memory Databases

There are two primary categories of database workloads that can suffer from delayed access to data. In-memory databases can help in both cases.

Online Transaction Processing (OLTP)

OLTP workloads are characterized by a high volume of low-latency operations that touch relatively few records. OLTP performance is bottlenecked by random data access—how quickly the system finds a given record and performs the desired operation. Conventional databases can capture moderate transaction levels, but trying to query the data simultaneously is nearly impossible. That has led to a range of separate systems focusing on analytics more than transactions. These online analytical processing (OLAP) solutions complement OLTP solutions.

However, in-memory solutions can increase OLTP transactional throughput; each transaction—including the mechanisms to persist the data—is accepted and acknowledged faster than a disk-based solution. This speed enables OLTP and OLAP systems to converge in a hybrid, or HTAP, system.

When building real-time applications, being able to quickly store more data in-memory sets a foundation for unique digital experiences such as a faster and more personalized mobile application, or a richer set of data for business intelligence.

Online Analytical Processing (OLAP)

OLAP becomes the system for analysis and exploration, keeping the OLTP system focused on capture of transactions. Similar to OLTP, users also seek speed of processing and typically focus on two metrics:

- *Data latency* is the time it takes from when data enters a pipeline to when it is queryable.
- *Query latency* represents the rate at which you can get answers to your questions to generate reports faster.

Traditionally, OLAP has not been associated with operational workloads. The "online" in OLAP refers to interactive query speed, meaning an analyst can send a query to the database and it returns in some reasonable amount of time (as opposed to a long-running "job" that may take hours or days to complete). However, many modern applications rely on real-time analytics for things like personalization and traditional OLAP systems have been unable to meet this need. Addressing this kind of application requires rethinking expectations of analytical data processing systems. In-memory analytical engines deliver the speed, low latency, and throughput needed for real-time insight.

HTAP: Bringing OLTP and OLAP Together

When working with transactions and analytics independently, many challenges have already been solved. For example, if you want to focus on just transactions, or just analytics, there are many existing database and data warehouse solutions:

- If you want to load data very quickly, but only query for basic results, you can use a stream processing framework.
- And if you want fast queries but are able to take your time loading data, many columnar databases or data warehouses can fit that bill.

However, rapidly emerging workloads are no longer served by any of the traditional options, which is where new HTAP-optimized architectures provide a highly desirable solution. HTAP represents a combination of low data latency and low query latency, and is delivered via an in-memory database. Reducing both latency variables with a single solution enables new applications and real-time data pipelines across industries.

Modern Workloads

Near ubiquitous Internet connectivity now drives modern workloads and a corresponding set of unique requirements. Database systems must have the following characteristics:

Ingest and process data in real-time
    In many companies, it has traditionally taken one day to understand and analyze data from when the data is born to when it is usable to analysts. Now companies want to do this in real time.

Generate reports over changing datasets
    The generally accepted standard today is that after collecting data during the day and not necessarily being able to use it, a four- to six-hour process begins to produce an OLAP cube or materialized reports that facilitate faster access for analysts. Today, companies expect queries to run on changing datasets with results accurate to the last transaction.

Anomaly detection as events occur
The time to react to an event can directly correlate with the financial health of a business. For example, quickly understanding unusual trades in financial markets, intruders to a corporate network, or the metrics for a manufacturing process can help companies avoid massive losses.

Subsecond response times
When corporations get access to fresh data, its popularity rises across hundreds to thousand of analysts. Handling the serving workload requires memory-optimized systems.

The Need for HTAP-Capable Systems

HTAP-capable systems can run analytics over changing data, meeting the needs of these emerging modern workloads. With reduced data latency, and reduced query latency, these systems provide predictable performance and horizontal scalability.

In-Memory Enables HTAP

In-memory databases deliver more transactions and lower latencies for predictable service level agreements or SLAs. Disk-based systems simply cannot achieve the same level of predictability. For example, if a disk-based storage system gets overwhelmed, performance can screech to a halt, wreaking havoc on application workloads.

In-memory databases also deliver analytics as data is written, essentially bypassing a batched extract, transform, load (ETL) process. As analytics develop across real-time and historical data, in-memory databases can extend to columnar formats that run on top of higher capacity disks or flash SSDs for retaining larger datasets.

Common Application Use Cases

Applications driving use cases for HTAP and in-memory databases range across industries. Here are a few examples.

Real-Time Analytics

Agile businesses need to implement tight operational feedback loops so decision makers can refine strategies quickly. In-memory databases support rapid iteration by removing conventional database bottlenecks like disk latency and CPU contention. Analysts appreciate the ability to get immediate data access with preferred analysis and visualization tools.

Risk Management

Successful companies must be able to quantify and plan for risk. Risk calculations require aggregating data from many sources, and companies need the ability to calculate present risk while also running ad hoc future planning scenarios.

In-memory solutions calculate volatile metrics frequently for more granular risk assessment and can ingest millions of records per second without blocking analytical queries. These solutions also serve the results of risk calculations to hundreds of thousands of concurrent users.

Personalization

Today's users expect tailored experiences and publishers, advertisers, and retailers can drive engagement by targeting recommendations based on users' history and demographic information. Personalization shapes the modern web experience. Building applications to deliver these experiences requires a real-time database to perform segmentation and attribution at scale.

In-memory architectures scale to support large audiences, converge a system or record with a system of insight for tighter feedback loops, and eliminate costly pre-computation with the ability to capture and analyze data in real time.

Portfolio Tracking

Financial assets and their value change in real time, and the reporting dashboards and tools must similarly keep up. HTAP and in-memory systems converge transactional and analytical processing so portfolio value computations are accurate to the last trade.

Now users can update reports more frequently to recognize and capitalize on short-term trends, provide a real-time serving layer to thousands of analysts, and view real-time and historical data through a single interface (Figure 1-1).

Figure 1-1. Analytical platform for real-time trade data

Monitoring and Detection

The increase in connected applications drove a shift from logging and log analysis to real-time event processing. This provides businesses the ability to instantly respond to events, rather than after the fact, in cases such as data center management and fraud detection. In-memory databases ingest data and run queries simultaneously, provide analytics on real-time and historical data in a single view, and provide the persistence for real-time data pipelines with Apache Kafka and Spark (Figure 1-2).

Figure 1-2. Real-time operational intelligence and monitoring

Conclusion

In the early days of databases, systems were designed to focus on each individual transaction and treat it as an atomic unit (for example, the debit and credit for accounting, the movement of physical inventory, or the addition of a new employee to payroll). These critical transactions move the business forward and remain a cornerstone of systems-of-record.

Yet, a new model is emerging where the aggregate of all the transactions becomes critical to understanding the shape of the business (for example, the behavior of millions of users across a mobile phone application, the input from sensor arrays in Internet of Things (IoT) applications, or the clicks measured on a popular website). These modern workloads represent a new era of transactions requiring in-memory databases to keep up with the volume of real-time data and the interest to understand that data in real time.

CHAPTER 2

First Principles of Modern In-Memory Databases

Our technological race to the future with billions of mobile phones, an endless stream of online applications, and everything connected to the Internet has rendered a new set of modern workloads. Our ability to handle these new data streams relies on having the tools to handle large volumes of data quickly across a variety of data types. In-memory databases are key to meeting that need.

The Need for a New Approach

Traditional data processing infrastructures, particularly the databases that serve as a foundation for applications, were not designed for today's mobile, streaming, and online world. Conventional databases were designed around slow mechanical disk drives that cannot keep up with modern workloads. Conventional databases were also designed as monolithic architectures, making them hard to scale, and forcing customers into expensive and proprietary hardware purchases.

A new class of in-memory solutions provides an antidote to legacy approaches, delivering peak performance as well as capabilities to enhance existing and support new applications.

For consumers, this might mean seeing and exchanging updates with hundreds or thousands of friends simultaneously. For business users, it might mean crunching through real-time and historical data simultaneously to derive insight on critical business decisions.

Architectural Principles of Modern In-Memory Databases

To tackle today's workloads and anticipate the needs of the future, modern in-memory databases adopt a set of architectural principles that distinctly separate them from traditional databases. These first principles include:

In-memory
Including the ability to accept transactions directly into memory

Distributed
Such that additional CPU horsepower and memory can be easily added to a cluster

Relational and multimodel
Relational to support interactive analytics, but also formats to support semi-structured data

Mixed media
Specifically the ability to use multiple types of storage media types such as integrated disk or flash for longer term storage

In-Memory

Memory, specifically RAM, provides speed levels hundreds of times faster than typical solid state drives with flash, and thousands of times faster than rotating disk drives made with magnetic media. As such, RAM is likely to retain a sweet spot for in-memory processing as a primary media type. That does not preclude incorporating combinations of RAM and flash and disk, as discussed later in this section.

But there are multiple ways to deploy RAM for in-memory databases, providing different levels of flexibility. In-memory approaches generally fit into three categories: memory after, memory only, and memory optimized (Figure 2-1). In these approaches we delineate where the database stores active data in its primary format. Note that this is different from logging data to disk, which is used for data protection and recovery systems and represents a separate process.

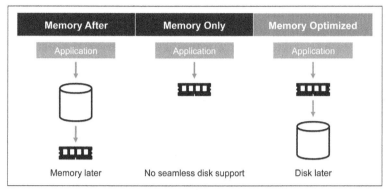

Figure 2-1. Differing types of in-memory approaches

Memory after

Memory-after architectures typically retain the legacy path of committing transactions directly to disk, then quickly staging them "after" to memory. This approach provides speed after the fact, but does not account for rapid ingest.

Memory only

A memory-only approach exclusively uses memory, and provides no native capability to incorporate other media types such as flash or disk. Memory-only databases provide performance for smaller datasets, but fail to account for the large data volumes common in today's workloads and therefore provide limited functionality.

Memory optimized

Memory-optimized architectures allow for the capture of massive ingest streams by committing transactions to memory first, then persisting to flash or disk following. Of course, options exist to commit every transaction to persistent media. Memory-optimized approaches allow all data to remain in RAM for maximum performance, but also for data to be stored on disk or flash where it makes sense for a combination of high volumes and cost-effectiveness.

Distributed Systems

Another first principle of modern in-memory databases is a distributed architecture that scales performance and memory capacity across a number of low-cost machines or cloud instances. As memory can be a finite resource within a single server, the ability to aggregate across servers removes this capacity limitation and provides cost advantages for RAM adoption using commodity hardware. For example, a two-socket web server costs thousands of dollars, while a scale-up appliance could cost tens to hundreds of thousands of dollars.

Relational with Multimodel

For in-memory databases to reach broad adoption, they need to support the most familiar data models. The relational data model, in particular the Structured Query Language (SQL) model, dominates the market for data workflows and analytics.

SQL

While many distributed solutions discarded SQL in their early days —consider the entire NoSQL market—they are now implementing SQL as a layer for analytics. In essence, they are reimplementing features that have existed in relational databases for many years.

A native SQL implementation will also support full transactional SQL including inserts, updates, and deletes, which makes it easy to build applications. SQL is the universal language for interfacing with common business intelligence tools.

Other models

As universal as SQL may be, there are times when it helps to have other models (Figure 2-2). JavaScript Object Notation (JSON) supports semi-structured data. Another relevant data type is geospatial, an essential part of the mobile world as today every data point has a location.

Completing the picture for additional data models is Spark, a popular data processing framework that incorporates a set of rich programming libraries. In-memory databases that extend to and incorporate Spark can provide immediate access to this functionality.

Since Spark itself does not include a persistence layer, in-memory databases that provide a high-throughput, parallel connector become a powerful persistent complement to Spark. Spark is explored in more detail in Chapter 5.

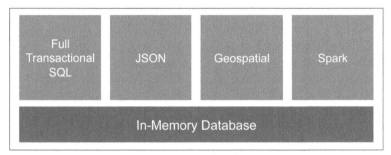

Figure 2-2. A multimodel in-memory database

Mixed Media

Understandably, not every piece of data requires in-memory placement forever. As data ages, retention still matters, but there is typically a higher tolerance to wait a bit longer for results. Therefore it makes sense for any in-memory database architecture to natively incorporate alternate media types like disk or flash.

One method to incorporate disk or flash with in-memory databases is through columnar storage formats. Disk-based data warehousing solutions typically deploy column-based formats and these can also be integrated with in-memory database solutions.

Conclusion

As with choices in the overall database market, in-memory solutions span a wide range of offerings with a common theme of memory as a vehicle for speed and agility. However, an in-memory approach is fundamentally different from a traditional disk-based approach and requires a fresh look at longstanding challenges.

Powerful solutions will not only deliver maximum scale and performance, but will retain enterprise approaches such as SQL and relational architectures, support application friendliness with flexible schemas, and facilitate integration into the vibrant data ecosystem.

CHAPTER 3

Moving from Data Silos to Real-Time Data Pipelines

Providing a modern user experience at scale requires a streamlined data processing infrastructure. Users expect tailored content, short load times, and information to always be up-to-date. Framing business operations with these same guiding principles can improve their effectiveness. For example, publishers, advertisers, and retailers can drive higher conversion by targeting display media and recommendations based on users' history and demographic information. Applications like real-time personalization create problems for legacy data processing systems with separate operational and analytical data silos.

The Enterprise Architecture Gap

A traditional data architecture uses an OLTP-optimized database for operational data processing and a separate OLAP-optimized data warehouse for business intelligence and other analytics. In practice, these systems are often very different from one another and likely come from different vendors. Transferring data between systems requires ETL (extract, transform, load) (Figure 3-1).

Legacy operational databases and data warehouses ingest data differently. In particular, legacy data warehouses cannot efficiently handle one-off inserts and updates. Instead, data must be organized into large batches and loaded all at once. Generally, due to batch size and rate of loading, this is not an online operation and runs overnight or at the end of the week.

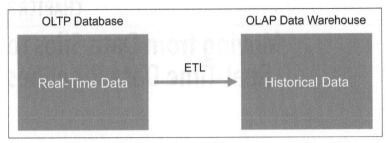

Figure 3-1. Legacy data processing model

The challenge with this approach is that fresh, real-time data does not make it to the analytical database until a batch load runs. Suppose you wanted to build a system for optimizing display advertising performance by selecting ads that have performed well recently. This application has a transactional component, recording the impression and charging the advertiser for the impression, and an analytical component, running a query that selects possible ads to show to a user and then ordering by some conversion metric over the past x minutes or hours.

In a legacy system with data silos, users can only analyze ad impressions that have been loaded into the data warehouse. Moreover, many data warehouses are not designed around the low latency requirements of a real-time application. They are meant more for business analysts to query interactively, rather than computing programmatically generated queries in the time it takes a web page to load.

On the other side, the OLTP database should be able to handle the transactional component, but, depending on the load on the database, probably will not be able to execute the analytical queries simultaneously. Legacy OLTP databases, especially those that use disk as the primary storage medium, are not designed for and generally cannot handle mixed OLTP/OLAP workloads.

This example of real-time display ad optimization demonstrates the fundamental flaw in the legacy data processing model. Both the transactional and analytical components of the application must complete in the time it takes the page to load and, ideally, take into account the most recent data. As long as data remains siloed, this will be very challenging. Instead of silos, modern applications require real-time data pipelines in which even the most recent data is always available for low-latency analytics.

Real-Time Pipelines and Converged Processing

Real-time data pipelines can be implemented in many ways and it will look different for every business. However, there are a few fundamental principles that must be followed:

1. Data must be processed and transformed "on the fly" so that, when it reaches a persistent data store, it is immediately available for query.
2. The operational data store must be able to run analytics with low latency.
3. Converge the system of record with the system of insight.

On the second point, note that the operational data store need not replace the full functionality of a data warehouse—this may happen, but is not required. However, to enable use cases like the real-time display ad optimization example, it needs to be able to execute more complex queries than traditional OLTP lookups.

One example of a common real-time pipeline configuration is to use Kafka, Spark Streaming, and MemSQL together.

At a high level, Kafka, a message broker, functions as a centralized location for Spark to read from disparate data streams. Spark acts a transformation layer, processing and enriching data in micro batches. MemSQL serves as the persistent data store, ingesting processed data from Spark. The advantage of using MemSQL for persistence is twofold:

1. With its in-memory storage, distributed architecture, and modern data structures, MemSQL enables concurrent transactional and analytical processing.
2. MemSQL has a SQL interface and the analytical query surface area to support business intelligence.

Because data travels from one end of the pipeline to the other in seconds, analysts have access to the most recent data. Moreover, the pipeline, and MemSQL in particular, enable use cases like real-time display ad optimization. Impression data is queued in Kafka, preprocessed in Spark, then stored and analyzed in MemSQL. As a transactional system, MemSQL can process business transactions (charging advertisers and crediting publishers, for instance) in addition to powering and optimizing the ad platform.

In addition to enabling new applications, and with them new top-line revenue, this kind of pipeline can improve the bottom line as well. Using fewer, more powerful systems can dramatically reduce your hardware footprint and maintenance overhead. Moreover, building a real-time data pipeline can simplify data infrastructure. Instead of managing and attempting to synchronize many different systems, there is a single unified pipeline. This model is conceptually simpler and reduces connection points.

Stream Processing, with Context

Stream processing technology has improved dramatically with the rise of memory-optimized data processing tools. While leading stream processing systems provide some analytics capabilities, these systems, on their own, do not constitute a full pipeline. Stream processing tools are intended to be temporary data stores, ingesting and holding only an hour's or day's worth of data at a time. If the system provides a query interface, it only gives access to this window of data and does not give the ability to analyze the data in a broader historical context. In addition, if you don't know exactly what you're looking for, it can be difficult to extract value from streaming data. With a pure stream processing system, there is only one chance to analyze data as it flies by (see Figure 3-2).

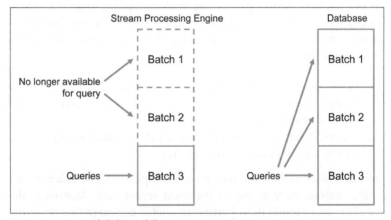

Figure 3-2. Availability of data in stream processing engine versus database

To provide access to real-time and historical data in a single system, some businesses employ distributed, high-throughput NoSQL data stores for "complex event processing" (CEP). These data stores can ingest streaming data and provide some query functionality. However, NoSQL stores provide limited analytic functionality, omitting common RDBMS features like joins, which give a user the ability to combine information from multiple tables. To execute even basic business intelligence queries, data must be transferred to another system with greater query surface area.

The NoSQL CEP approach presents another challenge in that it trades speed for data structure. Ingesting data as is, without a schema, makes querying the data and extracting value from it much harder. A more sophisticated approach is to structure data before it lands in a persistent data store. By the time data reaches the end of the pipeline, it is already in a queryable format.

Conclusion

There is more to the notion of a real-time data pipeline than "what we had before but faster." Rather, the shift from data silos to pipelines represents a shift in thinking about business opportunities. More than just being faster, a real-time data pipeline eliminates the distinction between real-time and historical data, such that analytics can inform business operations in real time.

CHAPTER 4

Processing Transactions and Analytics in a Single Database

The thought of running transactions and analytics in a single database is not completely new, but until recently, limitations in technology and legacy infrastructure have stalled adoption. Now, innovations in database architecture and in-memory computing have made running transactions and analytics in a single database a reality.

Requirements for Converged Processing

Converging transactions and analytics in a single database requires technology advances that traditional database management systems and NoSQL databases are not capable of supporting. To enable converged processing, the following features must be met.

In-Memory Storage

Storing data in memory allows reads and writes to occur orders of magnitude faster than on disk. This is especially valuable for running concurrent transactional and analytical workloads, as it alleviates bottlenecks caused by disk contention. In-memory operation is necessary for converged processing as no purely disk-based system will be able to deliver the input/output (I/O) required with any reasonable amount of hardware.

Access to Real-Time and Historical Data

In addition to speed, converged processing requires the ability to compare real-time data to statistical models and aggregations of historical data. To do so, a database must be designed to facilitate two kinds of workloads: (1) high-throughput operational and (2) fast analytical queries. With two powerful storage engines, real-time and historical data can be converged into one database platform and made available through a single interface.

Compiled Query Execution Plans

Without disk I/O, queries execute so quickly that dynamic SQL interpretation can become a bottleneck. This can be addressed by taking SQL statements and generating a compiled query execution plan. Compiled query plans are core to sustaining performance advantages for converged workloads. To tackle this, some databases will use a caching layer on top of their RDBMS. Although sufficient for immutable datasets, this approach runs into cache invalidation issues against a rapidly changing dataset, and ultimately results in little, if any, performance benefit. Executing a query directly in memory is a better approach, as it maintains query performance, even when data is frequently updated (Figure 4-1).

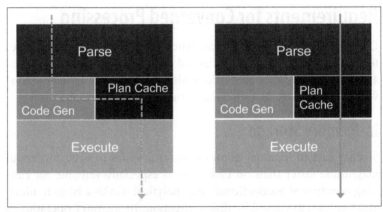

Figure 4-1. Compiled query execution plans

Granular Concurrency Control

Reaching the throughput necessary to run transactions and analytics in a single database can be achieved with lock-free data structures and multiversion concurrency control (MVCC). This allows the database to avoid locking on both reads and writes, enabling data to be accessed simultaneously. MVCC is especially critical during heavy write workloads such as loading streaming data, where incoming data is continuous and constantly changing (Figure 4-2).

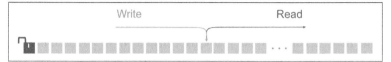

Figure 4-2. Lock-free data structures

Fault Tolerance and ACID Compliance

Fault tolerance and ACID compliance are prerequisites for any converged data processing systems, as operational data stores cannot lose data. To ensure data is never lost, a database should include redundancy in the cluster and cross-datacenter replication for disaster recovery. Writing database logs and complete snapshots to disk can also be used to ensure data integrity.

Benefits of Converged Processing

Many organizations are turning to in-memory computing for the ability to run transactions and analytics in a single database of record. For data-centric organizations, this optimized way of processing data results in new sources of revenue and a simplified computing structure that reduces costs and administrative overhead.

Enabling New Sources of Revenue

Many databases promise to speed up applications and analytics. However, there is a fundamental difference between simply speeding up existing business infrastructure and actually opening up new channels of revenue. True "real-time analytics" does not simply mean faster response times, but analytics that capture the value of data before it reaches a specified time threshold, usually some fraction of a second.

An example of this can be illustrated in financial services, where investors must be able to respond to market volatility in an instant. Any delay is money out of their pockets. Taking a single-database approach makes it possible for these organizations to respond to fluctuating market conditions as they happen, providing more value to investors.

Reducing Administrative and Development Overhead

By converging transactions and analytics, data no longer needs to move from an operational database to a siloed data warehouse or data mart to run analytics. This gives data analysts and administrators more time to concentrate efforts on business strategy, as ETL often takes hours, and in some cases longer, to complete.

Simplifying Infrastructure

By serving as a database of record and analytical warehouse, a hybrid database can significantly simplify an organization's data processing infrastructure by functioning as the source of day-to-day operational workloads.

There are many advantages to maintaining a simple computing infrastructure:

Increased uptime
A *simple* infrastructure has fewer potential points of failure, resulting in fewer component failures and easier problem diagnosis.

Reduced latency
There is no way to avoid latency when transferring data between data stores. Data transfer necessitates ETL, which is time consuming and introduces opportunities for error. The simplified computing structure of a converged processing database foregoes the entire ETL process.

Synchronization
With a hybrid database architecture, drill-down from analytic aggregates always points to the most recent application data. Contrast that to traditional database architectures where analytical and transactional data is siloed. This requires a cumbersome synchronization process and an increased likelihood that the "analytics copy" of data will be stale, providing a false representation of data.

Copies of data

In a converged processing system, the need to create multiple copies of the same data is eliminated, or at the very least reduced. Compared to traditional data processing systems, where copies of data must be managed and monitored for consistency, a single system architecture reduces inaccuracies and timing differences associated with data duplication.

Faster development cycles

Developers work faster when they can build on fewer, more versatile tools. Different data stores likely have different query languages, forcing developers to spend hours familiarizing themselves with the separate systems. When they also have different storage formats, developers must spend time writing ETL tools, connectors, and synchronization mechanisms.

Conclusion

Many innovative organizations are already proving that access to real-time analytics, and the ability to power applications with real-time data, brings a substantial competitive advantage to the table. For businesses to support emerging trends like the Internet of Things and the high expectations of users, they will have to operate in real time. To do so, they will turn to converged data processing, as it offers the ability to forego ETL and simplify database architecture.

CHAPTER 5

Spark

Background

Apache Spark is an open source cluster computing framework originally developed at UC Berkeley in the AMPLab. Spark is a fast and flexible alternative to both stream and batch processing systems like Storm and MapReduce, and can be integrated as a part of batch processing, stream processing, machine learning, and more. A recent survey of 2,100 developers revealed that 82% would choose Spark to replace MapReduce.

Characteristics of Spark

Spark is a versatile distributed data processing engine, providing a rich language for data scientists to explore data. It comes with an ever-growing suite of libraries for analytics and stream processing.

Spark Core consists of a programming interface and a distributed execution environment. On top of this core platform, the Spark developer community has built several libraries including Spark Streaming, MLlib (for machine learning), Spark SQL, and GraphX (for graph analytics) (Figure 5-1). As of version 1.3, Spark SQL was repackaged as the DataFrame API. Beyond acting as a SQL server, the DataFrame API is meant to provide a general purpose library for manipulating structured data.

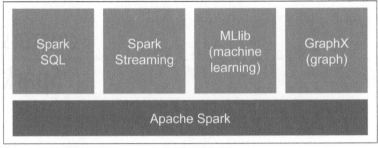

Figure 5-1. Spark data processing framework

The Spark execution engine keeps data in memory and has the ability to schedule jobs distributed over many nodes. Integrating Spark with other in-memory systems, like an in-memory database, facilitates efficient and quick operations.

By design, Spark is stateless—there is no persistent data storage. As such, Spark relies on other systems for serving, storing, and tracking changes to data. Spark can be used with a variety of external storage options including, most commonly, databases and filesystems. Different external data stores suit different use cases.

Understanding Databases and Spark

A common point of confusion is the relationship between Spark and databases. While there is some overlapping functionality, there are fundamental differences in design and functionality that distinguish the two. The most significant difference has already been mentioned: Spark is not a persistent data store.

Table 5-1 illustrates the similarities and differences between Spark and a relational database.

Table 5-1. Comparison between Spark and a relational database

	Relational database	Spark
Programming language	SQL	Scala and libraries
Execution environment	SQL engine, query optimizer	Distributed job scheduler
Persistent data storage	Yes	Relies on external databases and/or file systems
Data mutability	Transactional INSERT, UPDATE, DELETE	Datasets are immutable

Augmenting Spark with a real-time operational database opens a wide array of new use cases. With this setup, Spark can access live production data, and result sets from Spark can immediately be put to use in the database to support mission-critical applications. Pairing Spark with a real-time database enables companies to go from a static view to a dynamic view of operational metrics.

Spark's distributed, in-memory execution environment is one of its core innovations. In-memory data processing eliminates the disk I/O bottleneck, and the distributed architecture reduces CPU contention by enabling parallelized execution. Using Spark with a disk-optimized or single server database offsets the benefits of the Spark architecture (Figure 5-2).

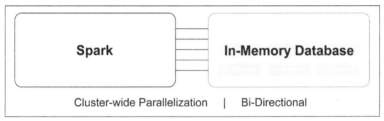

Figure 5-2. High throughput connectivity between an in-memory database and Spark

Other Use Cases

There are additional use cases for Spark beyond real-time streaming, for example, advanced analytics of operational data. Data scientists are often hindered by a lengthy and complex ETL process that limits instant access to fresh data. When Spark is connected to an operational database, fresh data can be loaded in Spark for analysis, then a simple write returns the results to the database, providing immediate query access to valuable real-time data.

Combining Spark with an operational database also enables businesses to go to production and iterate faster than ever by taking the results produced in Spark and putting them to immediate use.

Conclusion

Spark is an exciting technology that is changing the way businesses process and analyze data. More broadly, it reflects the trend toward scale-out, memory-optimized data processing systems. With use cases ranging from stream processing to machine learning, Spark also exemplifies the benefits of versatile, multipurpose infrastructure.

CHAPTER 6

Architecting Multipurpose Infrastructure

As data processing technology has matured, enterprise developers and architects have realized that one of the keys to scaling effectively is minimizing complexity. In the interest of limiting complexity, the trend in enterprise data architecture is moving toward using fewer, more versatile systems, rather than many narrow-purpose systems. In addition to complexity, adding systems requires more administration, hiring developers and administrators with more specialized skillsets, and more development work to glue all of the systems together.

The rise of NoSQL grew out of limitations in legacy RDBMS technology, specifically the lack of scalability and inability to handle semi-structured data. Suppose you're an AdTech company and you manage your business operations, like keeping track of funds available in active campaigns, in a relational database, but track clickstream data, whether or not a user clicked on an ad, in a NoSQL key-value store or document store.

Now suppose you want to analyze the effectiveness of a given campaign. In order to correlate dollars spent with conversions, you need to synthesize data coming from two different sources. This requires an additional aggregation layer, probably in your application. In addition to adding latency due to data transfer, this architecture requires writing a custom aggregation layer and, potentially, additional custom code for synchronizing data between the separate stores.

While introducing additional specialized systems may solve problems in the short run, over time the cost of complexity adds up. This chapter will cover trends in modern data processing systems that allow greater flexibility and more streamlined infrastructure. Topics include:

- "Multimodal" systems, which support more than one type of workload (such as OLTP and OLAP)
- "Multimodel" systems, which support more than one kind of logical data model
- Systems with tiered storage, enabling convergence of real-time and historical data

Even as data processing technology grows more powerful and versatile, this does not mean there is one single system that can or should be used for every data processing task.

Multimodal Systems

"Multimodal" refers to a system with multiple modes of operation. Commonly this refers to databases that support OLTP and OLAP workloads, but it could also include stream processing or complex event processing. The OLTP/OLAP example is the best understood and most represented in the market, and is discussed in greater depth in Chapter 4.

One point to consider when evaluating multimodal systems is whether the system can operate in both modes simultaneously. For instance, many databases both support transaction processing and offer analytic query functionality. However, their concurrency model effectively prevents the database from doing both simultaneously.

Multimodel Systems

"Multimodel" refers to a system that supports multiple data models. A data model specifies how data is logically organized and generally affects how data is serialized, stored, and queried. For example, most developers are familiar with the relational model, which represents data as keyed tuples (rows) of typed attributes (columns). Tuples are organized into groups called relations (tables). Other common data models include object relational, key-value, document, geospatial, and graph.

Different data models suit different types of data, depending on factors like attribute density, the availability of metadata like attribute types, and what you want to do with the data after collection. For example, business operations data, like sales or orders, generally fits well in a relational schema. All records will have the same "shape" since, for example, all sales occur at some time, for some price, between some buyer and some seller, and so forth.

In contrast, there are fewer guarantees about the structure of records for certain kinds of event processing. Suppose you're logging video playback information. Conceptually, it makes sense for each record to represent a session of the user watching a video. However, the attributes associated with sessions will likely be more varied than the sales example. Some users will pause the video, others will watch it straight through. Some users will experience video quality degradation, or may change the video resolution part way through. Recording a value for every possible session attribute, which would be necessary in a standard relational schema, will likely result in storing lots of NULLs.

This is why using multiple data stores with different data models may seem appealing. However, in many cases a preferable solution is to use a single data store that supports multiple data models. For example, some modern relational databases support a JSON data type. Document-oriented NoSQL databases commonly use JSON as a data format because it lends itself to representing semi-structured data. There is no enforced schema and it supports nested types.

Including a JSON type within a relational database allows users to store and query structured and semi-structured data together. Instead of building an additional processing layer for combining data from separate data store, users can query data in multiple formats with a single query (Figure 6-1).

```
+------+----------------+---------------+----------------------------------------------+
| id   | email          | name          | click_stream                                 |
+------+----------------+---------------+----------------------------------------------+
| 1561 | steven@email.com | steven jones | {"id":45,"is_active":true,"latitude":85.189408, |
|      |                |               | "longitude":45.897608, "tags":["memory",     |
|      |                |               | "database","query","performance","shard"],   |
|      |                |               | "clicked":[{"id":67,URI:"/photos"},{"id":89, |
|      |                |               | "URI":"/profile"}]}                          |
+------+----------------+---------------+----------------------------------------------+
| 4652 | pamela@email.com | pamela johns | {"id":84,"is_active":true,"latitude":80.456821, |
|      |                |               | "longitude":65.846521, "tags":["memory",     |
|      |                |               | "database","query","performance","shard"],   |
|      |                |               | "clicked":[{"id":67,URI:"/profile"},{"id":89, |
|      |                |               | "URI":"/product"}]}                          |
+------+----------------+---------------+----------------------------------------------+
```

Figure 6-1. In this example, `click_stream` *is a JSON column*

A query that touches both structured and semi-structured data may look something like this:

```
SELECT * FROM accounts WHERE click_stream::%is_active AND
JSON_LENGTH(click_stream::clicked) > 1;
```

Tiered Storage

Increasingly, modern data stores support multiple storage media, including DRAM (main memory), flash, and spinning disk. DRAM has established itself as the medium of choice for fast read and write access, especially for OLTP workloads. However, despite drops in the price of memory in recent years, it is not feasible for most companies to store very large datasets totally in DRAM.

To address this common concern, some modern data stores offer multiple storage options spread across different media, as in Figure 6-2. For example, some databases allow the user to transparently specify which data resides in memory or on disk on a per-table basis. Other databases support multiple storage media, but do not transparently expose those options to the user.

Note that storing some data in memory and some on flash or disk is not necessarily the same as tiered storage. For instance, some vendors have added in-memory analytical caches on top of their existing disk-based offering. An in-memory analytical cache can accelerate query execution, but does not provide true storage tiering since the in-memory copy of data is redundant.

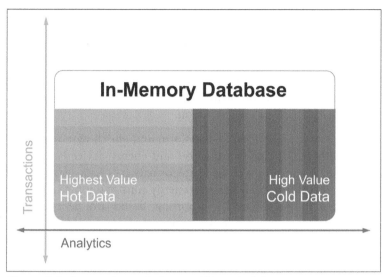

Figure 6-2. Converging real-time and historical data

The Real-Time Trinity: Apache Kafka, Spark, and an Operational Database

One of the most popular use cases for Spark is real-time stream and event processing. For example, the data science team at Pinterest uses Apache Kafka, Spark Streaming, and MemSQL, a combination that has been dubbed the "Real-Time Trinity," to ingest tens of thousands of events per second and aggregate that event data, which in this case is pins and repins (Figure 6-3). Kafka serves as the message queue, Spark provides the transformation tier, and the operational database offers data persistence and a serving layer for an application that allows for quick analysis of real-time trending topics by geography.

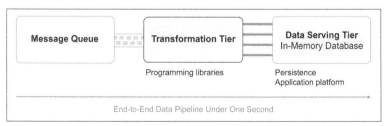

Figure 6-3. High-throughput real-time pipeline

Another example of the Real-Time Trinity is MemCity, a smart energy collection showcase. MemCity tracks, processes, and analyzes data from various energy devices that can be found in homes, measured by the minute in real time. It is built with the same architecture that Pinterest leverages: Kafka, Spark, and an operational database, to solve the problem of how to ingest, process, and serve real-time data across an organization.

In this case, Spark is used to transform and enrich data read from Kafka with geolocation information and energy device type information. The end result of this transformation is data served in an operational database to power live energy consumption dashboards. An image of the MemCity reporting dashboard generated by Tableau is shown in Figure 6-4. For organizations trying to plan for smart cities and sustainable energy consumption, this simulation highlights the importance of understanding data through real-time big data analytics.

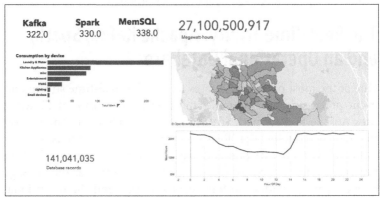

Figure 6-4. MemCity reporting dashboard generated by Tableau

Conclusion

In data processing infrastructure, simplicity and efficiency go hand in hand. Every system in a pipeline adds connection points, data transfer, and different data formats and APIs. While there is no single system that can manage all data processing needs for a modern enterprise, it is important to select versatile tools that allow a business to limit infrastructure complexity and to build efficient, resilient data pipelines.

CHAPTER 7

Getting to Operational Systems

Operational systems are at times mistakenly conflated with online transaction processing (OLTP) systems. They are in fact not the same. While operational systems process day-to-day transactions similarly to OLTP systems, they can also perform batch processing similarly to online analytical processing (OLAP) systems. An operational system is the system that processes daily transactions, but its use does not end there. The appropriate operational system for your enterprise can also enable real-time analysis, reporting, and decision making.

Getting to that ideal operational system requires choosing the appropriate technological components. Modern technology available today makes the choice simpler. It is important to consider several guiding principles.

Have Fewer Systems Doing More

There are two schools of thought here around this subject—"best of breed" and "consolidation." You will typically hear various vendors speak differently about both these approaches.

With the "best of breed" approach, you can add or remove components to or from your system, and ensure that only the "best" software for each of your needs are in your architecture. This example works well in theory, and promises that you will always have the best software for all your use cases without getting locked into one vendor. The reality is that in many cases the "best of breed" software solution for one usage scenario does not integrate well with the "best of breed" solution for your other usage scenarios. Their APIs don't play nicely together, their data models are very different, or they have vastly different interfaces such that you have to train your organization multiple times to use the system. The "best of breed" approach is also not maintainable over time unless you have strictly defined interfaces between your systems. Many companies end up resorting to middleware solutions to integrate the sea of disparate systems, effectively adding another piece of software on top of their growing array of solutions.

The other way companies think about operational systems is "consolidation." With this approach, you choose the least amount of software solutions that maximize the use cases covered. The "best of breed" school would argue that this causes vendor lock-in and over-reliance on one solution that may become more expensive over time. That said, that argument really only works on software solutions that have proprietary interfaces that are not transferrable to other systems. A counterexample for this is a SQL-based relational database using freely available client drivers. Enterprises should choose solutions that use interfaces where knowledge about their usage is generally available and widely applicable, and that can handle a vast amount of use cases. Consolidating your enterprise around systems such as these reduces vendor lock-in, allows you to use fewer systems to do more things, and makes maintenance over time much easier than the best of breed alternative. This is not to say that the ideal enterprise architecture would be to use only one system; that is unrealistic. Enterprises should, however, seek to consolidate software solutions when appropriate.

Modern Technologies Enable Real-Time Programmatic Decision Making

Until recently, limitations in database technology forced developers to separate transaction processing and analytical data processing, both physically and conceptually. The "online" in online analytical processing (OLAP) refers to queries executing at interactive speed. However, the data itself remains largely static, except for period batch updates, which usually happen at off-peak hours (overnight, for example). The result is that operations and analytics are decoupled.

Converging operational and analytical data processing not only creates tighter reporting feedback loops, but allows applications to programmatically use the results of real-time analysis. To illustrate the building of a modern operational system that handles the HTAP use case, let's consider the example of an ad serving platform.

The purpose of an ad serving platform is to optimize user engagement with display advertising. A common implementation is shown on the lefthand side of Figure 7-1.

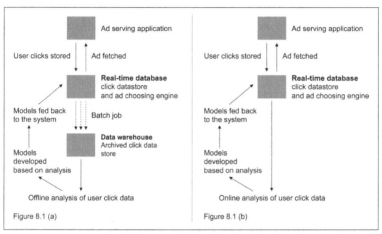

Figure 7-1. Ad serving platform architecture example: (a) traditional enterprise architecture and (b) modern enterprise architecture

Legacy enterprise architectures have two systems for data storage—an operational database and a non-real-time data warehouse. The operational database powers the platform, tracking impressions and clicks, as well as campaign targets and budgets. Adding analytics capabilities to the operational database, without blocking transactional throughput, enables more sophisticated targeting and optimization.

Consider an advertising platform that, in addition to using targeting algorithms, can analyze recent ad and campaign performance. For example, the platform may use a targeting algorithm to choose a set of possible ads to show, then run another query to determine how each of those possible ads have been performing recently, and choose one that has achieved a high conversion rate.

This application of real-time analytics is programmatic in that the platform acts autonomously, without input from a human, leveraging recent data to drive higher engagement. This kind of optimization is conceptually simple—using a relational database, the application can execute a query that orders results by some conversion metric. However, this would not be possible in a legacy system where operational data processing and analytics are separated by an offline ETL job and are siloed in separate data stores.

With a legacy system, the best case scenario is that an analyst notices that some ads are performing better and updates the targeting model, and the updated model is deployed to production days or even weeks later. In the interim, the ad serving platform continues selecting ads without preference for higher conversion rate. In contrast, a modern system that incorporates analytics into the serving process programmatically optimizes campaigns immediately, and drives better engagement, which means more revenue.

The ability to programmatically leverage real-time analytics has many applications within and beyond the digital advertising space. For instance, it could be used to optimize a financial trading platform by tracking real-time changes in pricing, or to manage a shipping network using real-time traffic information.

A proper database that can serve as both a real-time database and data warehouse should satisfy the following use cases, which usually translate to certain database features, as summarized in Table 7-1 below.

Table 7-1. Characteristics of databases that can serve as both a real-time database and data warehouse

Characteristic	Database feature
The database must handle high amounts of traffic.	Ability to scale out on commodity hardware, allowing massive parallelism of database transactions.
Data serving must happen in real time.	Database must have an in-memory component for maximum performance.
The database must hold both real-time and historical data.	Database should have a disk-based component that allows storage of large amounts of data.
The database should handle both simple and complex queries for programmatic analysis	Database should have a robust programmatic interface such as SQL.
Data analysis must not block or slow down data ingest.	Database readers must not block writers (and vice versa), while maintaining transactional consistency.

Modern Technologies Enable Ad-Hoc Reporting on Live Data

It is commonly thought that generating reports on a large data set always requires a preprocessing stage in another system for faster ad-hoc querying. Ad-hoc querying is defined as running queries individually on demand to derive insight on the current state of the system. The alternative to ad-hoc queries would be running queries repeatedly as part of a software application. Those queries are typically more performant, as both the underlying database system and query itself are properly optimized before being run.

This preprocessing stage for ad-hoc queries typically begins with a batch job moving data into another system, followed by several pre-processing steps for the data in the other system that aggregate the data or modify its representation (e.g., row store to column store conversion).

With modern systems, the need for standing up a separate system specifically for ad-hoc queries is no longer necessary.

To illustrate the building of a modern operational system that allows ad-hoc reporting without requiring a separate system, let's consider an Internet of Things (IoT) use case that will likely be increasingly common in a few years—a "smart city" (Figure 7-2). A smart city application measures and maps electric consumption across all households in a city. It tracks, processes, and analyzes data from various energy devices that can be found in homes, measured in real time.

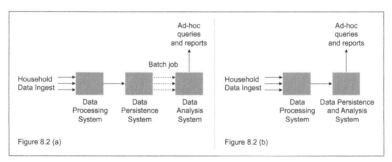

Figure 7-2. Smart city application architecture example: (a) traditional enterprise architecture and (b) modern enterprise architecture

As shown on the left side of Figure 7-2, smart city applications built with a traditional architecture would typically have a data processing system that can ingest large amounts of geotagged household data, a data persistence system that can reliably persist the volume of incoming data, and a data analysis system from which ad-hoc queries and reports can be built.

As shown on the right side of Figure 7-2, modern architectures do not rely on separate data persistence and data analysis systems. Instead, they allow ad-hoc queries to be run against the same system that provides the data persistence tier. As such, reliance on batch jobs to move data into a separate tier for reporting is unnecessary.

Conclusion

Modern technology makes it possible for enterprises to build the ideal operational system. To develop an optimally architected operational system, enterprises should look to use fewer systems doing more, to use systems that allow programmatic decision making on both real-time and historical data, and use systems that allow fast ad-hoc reporting on live data.

CHAPTER 8

Data Persistence and Availability

Fundamental to any operational database is its ability to store information durably and be resilient to unexpected machine failures. In more technical terms, an operational database must:

- Persist all its information to disk storage for durability.
- Ensure data is highly available by maintaining a readily available second copy of all data, and automatically failover without downtime in case of server crashes.

The previous chapters have been touting the ability of in-memory, distributed, SQL-based (relational) databases to provide the fastest performance for a wide amount of use cases, but the data persistence question always arises:

> If the database is "in-memory," what guarantees are there that the data will be fully persistent and always available?

This section will dive deep into the details of in-memory, distributed, SQL relational database systems and how they can be architected to guarantee data durability and high availability. Figure 8-1 presents a high-level architecture that illustrates how an in-memory database could provide these guarantees.

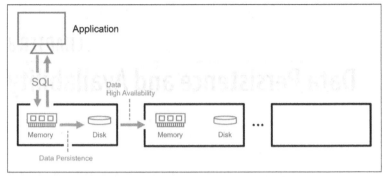

Figure 8-1. In-memory database persistence and high availability

Data Durability

For data storage to be durable, it must survive in the event of a server failure. After the server failure, the data should be recoverable into a transactionally consistent state without any data loss or corruption. In-memory databases guarantee this by periodically flushing snapshots of the in-memory store into a durable copy on disk, maintaining transaction logs, and replaying the snapshot and transaction logs upon server restart.

It is easier to understand data durability in an in-memory database through a specific scenario. Suppose a database application inserts a new record into a database. The following events will occur once a commit is issued:

1. The inserted record will be written to the in-memory data store.
2. A log of the transaction will be stored in a transaction log buffer in memory.
3. Once the transaction log buffer is filled, its contents are flushed to disk.
   a. The size of the transaction log buffer is configurable, so if it is set to 0, the transaction log will be flushed to disk after each committed transaction. This is also known as synchronous durability.
4. Periodically, full snapshots of the database are taken and written to disk.
   a. The number of snapshots to keep on disk, and the size of the transaction log at which a snapshot is taken, are configurable. Reasonable defaults are typically set.

Numerous settings to control the extent of data persistence are provided to the user. A user can choose to configure the database to be fully persisted to disk each time (synchronous durability), not be durable at all, or anywhere in between. The proper choice comes down to a trade-off between having a data loss window of zero and optimal performance. In-memory database users in financial services—where data persistence is very important—typically configure their systems closer to synchronous durability. On the other hand, in-memory database users dealing with sensor or clickstream data—where analytic speed is the priority—typically configure their systems with a higher transaction buffer window. Users tend to find a balance between the two by tuning the database levers appropriately.

Data Availability

Almost all the time, the requirements around data loss in a database are not focused on the data remaining fully durable in a single machine. The requirements are simply about the data remaining available and up-to-date at all times in the system as a whole. In other words, in a multimachine system, it is perfectly fine for data to be lost in one of the machines, as long as the data is still persisted somewhere in the system, and upon querying the data, it still returns a transactionally consistent result. This is where high availability comes in. For data to be highly available, it must be queryable from a system despite failures from some of the machines in the system.

It is easier to understand high availability through a specific scenario. In a distributed system, any number of machines in the system can fail. If a failure occurs, the following should happen:

1. The machine is marked as failed throughout the system.
2. A second copy of data in the failed machine, already existing in another machine, is promoted to be the "master" copy of data.
3. The entire system fails over to the new "master'" data copy, thus removing any system reliance on data present in the failed system.
4. The system remains online (i.e., queryable) all throughout the machine failure and data failover times.
5. If the failed machine recovers, the machine is integrated back into the system.

A distributed database system that guarantees high availability also has mechanisms for maintaining at least two copies of the data in different machines at all times. These copies must be fully in sync while the database is online through proper database replication. Distributed databases have settings for controlling network timeouts and data window sizes for replication.

A distributed database system is also very robust. Failures of its different components are mostly recoverable, and machines are auto-added into the distributed database efficiently and without loss of service or much degradation of performance.

Finally, distributed databases should also allow replication of data across wide distances, typically to a disaster recovery center offsite. This process is called cross datacenter replication, and is provided by most in-memory, distributed, SQL databases.

Data Backups

In addition to providing data durability and high availability, databases also provide ways to manually or programmatically create backups for the databases. Creating a backup is typically done by issuing a command, which immediately creates on-disk copies of the current state of the database. These database backups can then be restored into an existing or new database instance in the future for historical analysis or kept for long-term storage.

Conclusion

Databases should always provide persistence and high availability mechanisms for their data. Enterprises should only look at databases that provide this functionality for their mission-critical systems. In-memory SQL databases that are available today provide these guarantees through mechanisms for data durability (snapshots, transaction logs), data availability (master/slave data copies, replication), and data backups.

CHAPTER 9

Choosing the Best Deployment Option

As data-driven organizations move away from "big iron" appliances to agile infrastructures that favor agility and flexibility to scale, IT departments face multiple options to meet real-time demands. In this chapter we will look at the deployment decisions to consider across bare metal, virtual machines and containers, and the cloud, as shown in Figure 9-1.

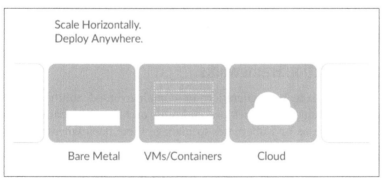

Figure 9-1. Flexible deployments for in-memory systems

Considerations for Bare Metal

Bare metal deployments provide the most direct access to the underlying hardware thereby maximizing performance on a per CPU or per GB of RAM basis. If new server purchases are required, bare metal environments can have a larger upfront cost, but they provide more cost-effective operation in the long run if the dataset and size remain relatively predictable.

Bare metal environments are mostly complemented by on-premises deployments, and in some cases cloud providers offer bare metal deployments.

Virtual Machine (VM) and Container Considerations

When working with a dataset and workload that require the agility and flexibility to scale as needed, virtual environments can be the right choice. Virtual machines offer many benefits such as fast server provisioning, fewer hardware restrictions, and easier migration to the cloud.

Containers are another option; they offer many of the benefits of virtual machines, but with a lighter approach since the operating system is not reprovisioned in every container. The result is faster and lighter weight deployments.

In some cases, companies might mandate the use of virtual machines without an option to deploy a bare metal server. In these cases, virtualization can still be deployed, but potentially with only one VM per physical machine. This provides the flexibility of a virtual environment but minimizes virtualization overhead by limiting each physical machine to one VM.

Orchestration Frameworks

With the recent proliferation of container-based solutions like Docker, many companies are choosing orchestration frameworks such as Mesos or Kubernetes to manage these deployments. Database architects seeking the most flexibility should evaluate these options; they can help when deploying different systems simultaneously that need to interact with each other, for example, a messaging queue, a transformation tier, and an in-memory database.

Considerations for Cloud or On-Premises Deployments

The right solution between cloud or on-premises deployments depends on several factors that may vary between companies and applications.

Benefits of Cloud: Expansion and Flexibility

When it comes to flexibility and ability to scale, cloud infrastructure has the advantage. Leveraging cloud deployments offers the ability to quickly scale out during peak workloads when higher performance is required, and scale back as needed. Cloud deployments also provide ease of expansion to new regions without the heavy overhead.

Contrast that with an on-premises data center that requires developers to account for peak workloads before they occur, leaving infrastructure investment underutilized during nonpeak times.

Benefits of On-Premises: Control, Security, Performance Optimization, and Predictability

While cloud computing offers easy startup costs and the ability to scale, many companies still retain large portions of data infrastructure on-premises for some of the following reasons.

Control

On-premises database systems provide the highest level of control over data processing and performance. The physical systems are all dedicated to their owner, as opposed to being shared on a cloud infrastructure. This eliminates being relegated to a lowest common denominator of performance and instead allows fine-tuned assignment of resources for performance-intensive applications.

Security

If your data is private or highly regulated, an on-premise database infrastructure may be the most straightforward option. Financial and government services and healthcare providers handle sensitive customer data according to complex regulations that are often more easily addressed in a dedicated on-site infrastructure.

Performance optimization and predictability

With more control over hardware, it is easier to maximize performance for a particular workload. At the same time, performance on premises is typically more predictable as it is not compromised by shared servers.

One area in particular where on-premises deployments can provide an advantage is networking. In a cloud environment, there is often little choice for network options, whereas on-premises architectures offer full control of the network environment.

Choosing the Right Storage Medium

Depending on data workload and use case, you will be faced with various options for how data is stored. There will likely be some combination of data being stored in memory and on SSD, and in some cases on disk.

RAM

When working with high-value, transactional data, RAM is the best option. RAM is orders of magnitude faster than SSD, and enables real-time processing and analytics on a changing dataset. For organizations with real-time data requirements, high-value data is kept in memory for a specified period of time and later moved to disk for historical analytics.

SSD and Disk

Solid state disks and conventional magnetic disks can be used to complement a RAM solution. To optimize for I/O, SSDs and disks perform best on sequential operations, such as logging for a RAM-based rowstore or storing data in a disk-based column store.

Deployment Conclusions

Perhaps the only certainty with computer systems is that things are likely to change. As applications evolve and data requirements expand, architects need to ensure that they can rapidly adopt.

Before choosing an in-memory architecture, be sure that it offers the flexibility to scale across a variety of deployment options. This will mitigate the risks of a changing system and provide the simplest means for continued operation.

CHAPTER 10

Conclusion

In-memory optimized databases are filling the gap where legacy relational database management systems and NoSQL databases have failed to deliver. By implementing a hybrid data processing model, organizations can obtain instant access to incoming data while gaining faster and more targeted insights. With the ability to process and analyze data as it is being generated, data-driven businesses can detect operational trends as they happen rather than reacting after the fact.

Recommended Next Steps

Now is the time to begin exploring in-memory options. Organizations with a focus on quickly deriving business value from emerging and growing data sources should identify data processing and storage solutions with in-memory storage, compiled query execution, enterprise-ready fault tolerance, and ACID compliance.

To get a competitive advantage from real-time data pipelines, we recommend the following:

- Identify real-time use cases within your organization, prioritizing by selecting processes that will either have the biggest revenue impact or that are easiest to implement.
- Investigate in-memory database solutions available in the market, giving preference to distributed systems that offer a memory optimized architecture.

- Explore leveraging open source frameworks such as Apache Kafka and Apache Spark to streamline data pipelines and enrich data for analysis.
- Select a vendor and run a proof of concept that puts your use case(s) to the test.
- Go to production at a manageable scale to validate the value of real-time analytics or applications.

There's no getting around the fact that the world is moving towards operating in real time. For your business, possessing the ability to analyze and react to incoming data will give you an upper hand that could be the difference between growth or stagnation. With technology advances such as in-memory computing and distributed systems, it's entirely possible to implement a cost-effective, high-performance data processing model that enables your business to operate at the pace and scale of incoming data. The question is, are you up for the challenge?

About the Authors

Gary Orenstein is the Chief Marketing Officer at MemSQL and leads marketing strategy, product management, communications, and customer engagement. Prior to MemSQL, Gary was the Chief Marketing Officer at Fusion-io, and also served as Senior Vice President of Products during the company's expansion to multiple product lines. Prior to Fusion-io, Gary worked at infrastructure companies on file systems, caching, and high-speed networking.

Conor Doherty is a Data Engineer at MemSQL, responsible for creating content around database innovation, analytics, and distributed systems. He also sits on the product management team, working closely on the Spark-MemSQL Connector. While Conor is most comfortable working on the command line, he occasionally takes time to write blog posts (and books) about databases and data processing.

Kevin White is the Director of Operations and a content contributor at MemSQL. He has worked at technology startups for more than 10 years, with a deep expertise in the Software-as-a-Service (SaaS) arena. Kevin is passionate about customer experience and growth with an emphasis on data-driven decision making.

Steven Camiña is a Principal Product Manager at MemSQL. His experience spans B2B enterprise solutions, including databases and middleware platforms. He is a veteran in the in-memory space, having worked on the Oracle TimesTen database. He likes to engineer compelling products that are user-friendly and drive business value.

CPSIA information can be obtained
at www.ICGtesting.com
Printed in the USA
FSOW03n1125021015
11779FS